2/02

Critical Acclaim for the poetry of Julia Alvarez
THE OTHER SIDE/EL OTRO LADO

Lucid. . . . Written with a novelist's sense of narrative and place, these poems forge ahead in language as plain and palpable as thick Caribbean light. . . . an affecting and genuine exploration laced with wisdom and humor. . . . Alvarez maps out the heart's ongoing journey . . . and the thin, precarious bridges we build from country to country, from silence, from childhood to whatever place we invent for ourselves in the world."   —*Miami Herald*

"Tracing a lyrical journey through the landscape of immigrant life, these direct, reflective, and often sensuous poems . . . take us across borders so slowly that only on reaching the other side can we see the distances we've come. . . . Meticulous . . . assured . . . Alvarez claims her authority as a poet with this collection."   —*Publishers Weekly*

"Playful and profound."—*San Francisco Chronicle Book Review*

JULIA ALVAREZ was born in the Dominican Republic and emigrated with her family to the United States in 1960. She is the author of another collection of poetry, *The Other Side/El Otro Lado*; her prize-winning, internationally bestselling first novel, *How the García Girls Lost Their Accents*; and her widely praised novel *In the Time of the Butterflies*, which was nominated for the 1995 National Book Critics Circle Award. All are available in Dutton and/or Plume editions. Ms. Alvarez is currently professor of English at Middlebury College.

HOMECOMING

New and Collected Poems

Julia Alvarez

A PLUME BOOK

For my parents and my family of friends

PLUME
Published by the Penguin Group
Penguin Books USA Inc., 375 Hudson Street, New York, New York 10014, U.S.A.
Penguin Books Ltd, 27 Wrights Lane, London W8 5TZ, England
Penguin Books Australia Ltd, Ringwood, Victoria, Australia
Penguin Books Canada Ltd, 10 Alcorn Avenue, Toronto, Ontario, Canada M4V 3B2
Penguin Books (N.Z.) Ltd, 182–190 Wairau Road, Auckland 10, New Zealand

Penguin Books Ltd, Registered Offices: Harmondsworth, Middlesex, England

Published by Plume, an imprint of Dutton Signet, a division of Penguin Books USA Inc.

First Plume Printing, March, 1996
10 9 8 7 6 5 4 3 2

The author gratefully acknowledges the editors of the following magazines and antholo-
gies in which these poems first appeared:
   American Poetry Review: "Redwing Sonnets," "Wallpaper"; *Calyx*: "Against Cin-
derella," "Making Our Beds"; *The Caribbean Review*: "Homecoming"; *Helicon Nine*:
"Sweeping"; *Men & Women: Together and Alone: The Spirit That Moves Us*: "Woman
Friend"; *New York Times*: "Woman's Work"; *Poetry*: "Heroines," "New Clothes"; *The Po-
etry Miscellany*: "Posture Lesson," "What Could It Be"; *13th Moon*: "Bedmaking,"
"Ironing Their Clothes," "Naming the Fabrics," "Orchids"; *Total Recall*: "Hairwashing";
WPFW 89.3 Poetry Anthology: "Dusting."

 REGISTERED TRADEMARK—MARCA REGISTRADA

LIBRARY OF CONGRESS CATALOGING-IN-PUBLICATION DATA:
Alvarez, Julia.
   Homecoming : new and collected poems / Julia Alvarez.
      p.   cm.
   ISBN 0-452-27567-9
   I. Title.
PS3551.L845H6   1996
811'.54—dc20   95-44118
                                                                                 CIP

Printed in the United States of America

Language is the only homeland.

—CZESLAW MILOSZ

CONTENTS

HOMECOMING

Homecoming

When my cousin Carmen married, the guards
at her father's *finca* took the guests' bracelets
and wedding rings and put them in an armored truck
for safekeeping while wealthy, dark-skinned men,
their plump, white women and spoiled children
bathed in a river whose bottom had been cleaned
for the occasion. She was Tío's only daughter,
and he wanted to show her husband's family,
a bewildered group of sunburnt Minnesotans,
that she was valued. He sat me at their table
to show off my English, and when he danced with me,
fondling my shoulder blades beneath my bridesmaid's gown
as if they were breasts, he found me skinny
but pretty at seventeen, and clever.
Come back from that cold place, Vermont, he said,
all this is yours! Over his shoulder
a dozen workmen hauled in blocks of ice
to keep the champagne lukewarm and stole
glances at the wedding cake, a dollhouse duplicate
of the family *rancho*, the shutters marzipan,
the cobbles almonds. A maiden aunt housekept,
touching up whipped cream roses with a syringe
of eggwhites, rescuing the groom when the heat
melted his chocolate shoes into the frosting.
On too much rum Tío led me across the dance floor,
dusted with talcum for easy gliding, a smell
of babies underfoot. He twirled me often,
excited by my pleas of dizziness, teasing me
that my merengue had lost its Caribbean.
Above us, Chinese lanterns strung between posts
came on and one snapped off and rose
into a purple postcard sky.

A grandmother cried: *The children all grow up too fast.*
The Minnesotans finally broke loose and danced a Charleston
and were pronounced good gringos with latino hearts.
The little sister, freckled with a week of beach,
her hair as blonde as movie stars, was asked
by maids if they could touch her hair or skin,
and she backed off, until it was explained to her,
they meant no harm. *This is all yours,*
Tío whispered, pressing himself into my dress.
The workmen costumed in their workclothes danced
a workman's jig. The maids went by with trays
of wedding bells and matchbooks monogrammed
with Dick's and Carmen's names. It would be years
before I took the courses that would change my mind
in schools paid for by sugar from the fields around us,
years before I could begin to comprehend
how one does not see the maids when they pass by
with trays of deviled eggs arranged in daisy wheels.
—It was too late, or early, to be wise—
The sun was coming up beyond the amber waves
of cane, the roosters crowed, the band struck up
Las Mañanitas, a morning serenade. I had a vision
that I blamed on the champagne:
the fields around us were burning. At last
a yawning bride and groom got up and cut
the wedding cake, but everyone was full
of drink and eggs, roast pig, and rice and beans.
Except the maids and workmen,
sitting on stoops behind the sugar house,
ate with their fingers from their open palms
windows, shutters, walls, pillars, doors,
made from the cane they had cut in the fields.

HOUSEKEEPING

How I Learned to Sweep

My mother never taught me sweeping.
One afternoon she found me watching
t.v. She eyed the dusty floor
boldly, and put a broom before
me, and said she'd like to be able
to eat her dinner off that table,
and nodded at my feet, then left.
I knew right off what she expected
and went at it. I stepped and swept;
the t.v. blared the news; I kept
my mind on what I had to do,
until in minutes, I was through.
Her floor was as immaculate
as a just-washed dinner plate.
I waited for her to return
and turned to watch the President,
live from the White House, talk of war:
in the Far East our soldiers were
landing in their helicopters
into jungles their propellers
swept like weeds seen underwater
while perplexing shots were fired
from those beautiful green gardens
into which these dragonflies
filled with little men descended.
I got up and swept again
as they fell out of the sky.
I swept all the harder when
I watched a dozen of them die.
as if their dust fell through the screen
upon the floor I had just cleaned.
She came back and turned the dial;

the screen went dark. *That's beautiful,*
she said, and ran her clean hand through
my hair, and on, over the window-
sill, coffee table, rocker, desk,
and held it up—I held my breath—
That's beautiful, she said, impressed,
she hadn't found a speck of death.

Dusting

Each morning I wrote my name
on the dusty cabinet, then crossed
the dining table in script, scrawled
in capitals on the backs of chairs,
practising signatures like scales
while Mother followed, squirting
linseed from a burping can
into a crumpled-up flannel.

She erased my fingerprints
from the bookshelf and rocker,
polished mirrors on the desk
scribbled with my alphabets.
My name was swallowed in the towel
with which she jeweled the table tops.
The grain surfaced in the oak
and the pine grew luminous.
But I refused with every mark
to be like her, anonymous.

Household Riddle

How did it go? Either
you dusted, then swept,
or reversed, you swept first
and then dusted, confused
for it seemed Mother changed
her mind on the order
each time she ordered
the sweeping then dusting,
or dusting then sweeping.

Like when there's lightning,
you stand under a tree
or was it an open field
in case the tree fell
it wouldn't hurt you?
Was it the cuffs first
when you were ironing
then the long stretch
of the back or vice versa?

Because if you dust first,
wouldn't you sweep back
the dust on the bureau top?
But if you swept first,
wouldn't you end up
with dust on the floor?
Which one went first?
Chicken-and-egg riddle!
Sphinx-like, my mother,
broom in one hand
and rag in the other,
waited to hear the right
wrong-sounding answer.

Making Our Beds

I

Mother does not approve of women brought up these days
who do not know their beds,
waterbed women, sleeping bag girls,
springs-on-the-floor Orphan Annies.
What mother would raise a daughter to sleep in the dust?
You're born on a bed, you die on a bed,
the most important things—
She eyed me, not yet, not yet—
will happen in bed.

II

This is the hospital corner, she said,
Lift up the top edge, tuck in the bottom,
bring down the top edge and tuck.
Good girl!

Her mammoth bed stood on mahogany claws.
She smoothed a blanket and tucked, I folded.
When I was a girl, I stood where you stand.
I daydreamed a girl in braids, taking my give.
Tuck, tuck, she scolded. I tucked, she folded.
Head in the clouds! She centered, I evened,
we each tucked our sides in.

Once or twice, hand cupped on a poster top,
she told me her story: *This was our wedding bed.*
Old enough, old enough, I scanned the sheets
for a spot of the stuff I was made of.

I tucked, she bent, we folded.
I will leave it for you.
But should I go first, she leaned over
to me on my side of the bed,
Don't let him put a strange woman—
She slapped flat a pillow—
in here where I gave him myself!

Bed by bed, we woke up the house, master bed first,
woke up the trundle beds, the four posters.
She fluffed each pillow up, patted each pucker down,
caught the mistake of the top sheet folded down seam up.
Take it all out! I groaned. She glared.
I rolled my eyes, color of hers, up.
You have it easy, finicky pea princess,
Fitted sheets, no-iron percale, imperial edges.
She waved her small hand. *Bring down the bedspreads!*

The bedspreads came down from their perches on bureaus,
unrolling their fussiness, their chintzes and cretonnes,
matching the curtains, the skirts of the vanity.
Mine was a sky of swans, wingtip to wingtip, blue and white organdy.
The bedwetting sisters had practical corduroy in practical brown,
a Noah's ark of stuffed animals dry at the head of their beds.
Hers was a print of a lady, cocking her parasol
at a gentleman, leering, in top hat and mustache.
Head to foot, left to right, over the edge
they flirted and fell to the brocatelle skirt.
Be careful you don't tuck the skirt in!

Sometimes I folded him closer
so his mustache tickled her chin and she smiled.
And I dreamed I was wife to this brocatelle husband.
Under my bed he breathed into life one night,
thumped at my back, mentioned unmentionable things.

I cried till she came in a flurry of light clicks.
In the blowing night she gathered the kicked-off covers,
docked the sailing curtains by clapping the windows closed.
This is what comes of a badly made bed!
We made the bed safe by making it over.

Once or twice, finger to lips, wise in her whispers,
she told me the secrets:
Don't sit on a made bed, you'll die an old maid.
Don't lay a man's coat on a bed, bad luck.
Tuck under your pillow at New Year's, a yes and a no.
In the morning reach under,
unfold the answer to love ...
her smile as coy as her brocatelle lady's.

III

I remember the hospital bed she bought for her bed-ridden mother
one night after supper. I came as her helper.
Past Christmas lights flashing their galaxies,
yards full of fir trees bleeding their resins,
we drove, I wiping her windows,
to the bad neighborhood where the Med Supply Outlet
sold bedpans and braces, crutches and motorized limbs
at reduced holiday prices.

She sat me up on that hospital bed,
lifted the guardrails,
cranked me high, cranked me low,
cranked me down to the three head-rest positions:
one for the patient's eating convenience,
one for relaxing, reading, and visiting,
one just a crank of the head above dying.

Over and over she queried the weary salesman.
He told her it came unassembled
and guaranteed for a year.
But do the rollers lock?
Back and forth he rolled me over the booming floor of the warehouse
and jerked to a stop. My head spun. . . .
I remembered the smell of my grandmother's bedding,
the feel of her thin arm pincushioned with needles.
We'll take her.

They strapped her to the rack of the car
while I waited, fumbling with dials.
The stations were crackling, spitting their static,
as I watched through the steamed up windows,
two shadowy figures securing the box with rods, tugging and knotting.
And the bulletin told of a blizzard to come,
the birth of a god, a little tin drum, three turtle doves.
That's that, she climbed in. *Pray that it holds!*
She waved at the good riddance salesman.
And away we roared, she giving it gas,
her mother's deathbed on the roof of the car
filling with new-falling snow.

IV

Night after night, she tucked me in,
folding the bedspread to the foot of the bed,
checking her tucking and tucking again.
She knew how a dream could take me.

Night after night, she sat midbed, making a crater,
touched with her mother palm all of me under the coverlet.
In an off-key voice, she wailed a lullaby
of a daughter buried alive by a stepmother.
An olive tree sprouted above the new grave
and sang,
>   *Oh Stepmother, have pity!*
I shivered. She patted the coverlet.

As the curtain swans soared in the summertime breezes,
she prayed to the Virgin, *Mother of God, Blessed among women.*
Night after night, her breath touched its quick to my quick
and my spirit lit up!
I fought the droop of my eyelids.
I strove to stay up with her voice in the darkness.
But I fell far away from her,
through bed by bed we had made that morning,
straining to listen—until I cannot remember.

The Master Bed

Mornings after my father left for work,
Mother and I made up the master bed.
She took everything off, down to the bottom sheet,
floated it up with a snap, centered, took in my give,
until that bed was modest in topsheet and blanket,
dressed up in bedspread, until that bed was done!

Sometimes the black nose of his slipper poked out
from under the bedskirt. Sometimes the long pillow
with a sultan's tassel at each end rolled down
from the head of the bed. Often I found crumpled Kleenex
or a wayward sock between sheets. Once a nosebleed
on her pillowcase. I wanted something shocking

to explain my being conceived of in that carpeted bedroom,
something we couldn't tidy though she'd try
to call it *love*. But I found nothing to inspire me—
only newspapers by his bedside, by hers a glass of warm water.
One sunbright morning in a shaft of light
a suspension of dust motes whirled like a primal moment.

Washing the Windows

I helped with the windows,
hosing them down,
while she plunged her sponge
into a soapy bucket
clouding them up.

She stretched for the top panes
and squatted on the ladder
level with my shoulder
for the low ones
I might have done.

I handed her the towels,
took them crumpled back
and grew bored
emptying her bucket,
giving her what she needed

up there on a ladder
too dangerous for a child.
Only when I aimed the hose up
making the glass drum and the suds scatter
did I get the feel of the job.

On the tip of her sneakers,
she made the high glasses
glow like mirrors
and lowered the sky back
into each window.

Storm Windows

She climbed toward the sky
when we did windows,
while I stood by, her helper,
doing the humdrum groundwork,
carrying her sloppy buckets
back and forth to the spigot,
hosing the glasses down
under her supervision
up there on a ladder
she had forbidden me.

I wanted to mount that ladder,
rung by rung, look down
into the gaping mouths of buckets,
the part in her greying hair.
I wanted to rise, polishing into each pane
another section of the sky.
Then give a kick, unbuckling
her hands clasped about my ankles,
and sail up, beyond her reach,
her house, her yard, her mothering.

Hairwashing

She washed my hair whenever I misbehaved,
ducking my head into a sink of water,
lathering up a head of old man's hair,
short quills, soft fur—
her porcupine, her bear,
her bad bad girl.
"Hold still!" she yelled.

I couldn't. I was growing up
even as she scrubbed for dirt,
horns, anything that looked like sin.
She could not clean inside the bowing head,
tidy the messy loves to come.
She could not set a quarantine on Eden
till she had found the serpent there.
She could not wring desire from my body
or take the curl out of my hair.

Hanging the Wash

My mother comes out the back door,
the ropes on her forearms taut.
She carries the wicker basket crammed with the first load,
dripping a dark trail on the concrete laundry yard.
She sets her burden down, shields her eyes,
studies the clouds, the willow boughs, then looks
down at her skirt to see which way the wind is blowing.

*

She bends
to her basket
and pulls out
her first piece,
puts it back,
rolls a white
cotton lump
over, tugs
at a long
something
or other—
No, that won't
do either.

She has in mind
a line in which
everything fits,
has room to inflate
to full shape
in the wind,
not a belt or a
shift or a panty
left over or back-
to-back towels or
socks doubled-up
or a dust rag draped
on a fencepost.

No wonder
she hesitates
before putting out
a line that must hold
all the clothes
in her basket.
Where to begin?
she wonders
looking about her
for any distraction
before she picks out
a dark fistful
of fabric

and lets it slowly
unravel and take
unmistakable shape
as she carefully
puts it where it
always belonged
on her washline.

*

A
sock
for
lorn
with
out
its
mate
heel
caved
in
longs
with
a
long
toe
for
the
earth
again.

*

Here comes its mate, pegged!
Rather on closer look, the mate
to a smaller, darker foot.
Mine! she thinks.

But she knows nothing
on the line can be owned.
Wholly dry, the wash swells
with the wind toward the sky.

*

Next to her husband's lumpy undershirt,
her bra seems sadly complicated:
lace cups,
          straps,
                    three choices
for
    the hook
            to eye.

*

The diaper squares are endless....
Does the baby know how to do
anything besides wet them
or drool on the bibs which follow?

*

The handkerchief she cried in
drips back into the ground her tears.

*

Oh, the democracy of a line of wash!
A first grade jumper flies up
leaving big sister's shorts behind.
Dad's limp drawers hang beside
Mom's blowing apron.
Liberated by a gust,
her wimpy nylons kick their heels up!

*

A tasseled belt
dangles
with sudden gusts
as if a great bell
in the heavens
were being tolled.

She imagines herself
years down the line:
skin wrinkled
like wrung cloth,
body shrunk
to clean bone.

*

What is that collapsed heap
she bodies with a hanger?
The whole misshapen shape weeps
until the breeze hits, spreading the pleats,
lifting her dress, high, high,
beyond the line, the house, the elms,
the willow boughs, the birds, the clouds.

*

On the line two crumpled gloves
slowly fill with ghostly hands;
thumbs and fingers feel the air
as if they meant to buy a yard.
Beside them a depleted skirt
gives her gathers to the wind,
then abandons any shame
and throws herself toward the sky!
The gloves reach out as if to touch
some privacy that's underneath.
But nothing's there—except the world:
willow, elm, washbasket, pegs,
a woman filling up the line
with laundry whose shapes suggest
loved ones, spotless, rising up
toward a promised paradise,
but, in a sudden lapse of wind,
descending to the only earth
there is to love another in.

She bends deeper into her basket,
ties and belts, accessories,
easily lost attachments,
a frivolous quintet of panties,
doilies which spider web the view,
a tablecloth, a row of napkins,
pajamas yawning with wind,
trousers prancing, a couple
of gutsy bras, shirts holding on
by their sleeves, four more handkerchiefs.
A mustache of sweat beads above her lip.
Her raised arms reveal two wet patches.

And yet, spotless, lazing on the line,
her wash basks in holiday sunshine.

Folding My Clothes

Tenderly she would take them down and fold
the arms in and fold again where my back
should go until she made a small
tight square of my chest, a knot of socks
where my feet blossomed into toes,
a stack of denim from the waist down,
my panties strictly packed into the size
of handkerchiefs on which no trace
of tears showed. All of me under control.

But there was tenderness, the careful matching
of arm to arm, the smoothing of wrinkles,
every button buttoned on the checkered blouse
I disobeyed in. There was sweet order
in those scented drawers, party dresses
perfect as pictures in the back of the closet—
until I put them on, breathing life back
into those abstract shapes of who I was
which she found so much easier to love.

Ironing Their Clothes

With a hot glide up, then down, his shirts,
I ironed out my father's back, cramped
and worried with work. I stroked the yoke,
the breast pocket, collar and cuffs,
until the rumpled heap relaxed into the shape
of my father's broad chest, the shoulders shrugged off
the world, the collapsed arms spread for a hug.
And if there'd been a face above the buttondown neck,
I would have pressed the forehead out, I would
have made a boy again out of that tired man!

If I clung to her skirt as she sorted the wash
or put out a line, my mother frowned,
a crease down each side of her mouth.
This is no time for love! But here
I could linger over her wrinkled bedjacket,
kiss at the damp puckers of her wrists
with the hot tip. Here I caressed
collars, scallops, ties, pleats which made
her outfits test of the patience of my passion.
Here I could lay my dreaming iron on her lap.

The smell of baked cotton rose from the board
and blew with a breeze out the window
to the family wardrobe drying on the clothesline,
all needing a touch of my iron. Here I could tickle
the underarms of my big sister's petticoat
or secretly pat the backside of her pajamas.
For she too would have warned me not to muss
her fresh blouses, starched jumpers, and smocks,
all that my careful hand had ironed out,
forced to express my excess love on cloth.

Rolling Dough

Mother lifted the roller, centered, and rolled,
biting her lip to avoid a tear in the strudel-thin dough.
I waited to hold the handles of the pin
and roll out the soft ball in my palm
into a big, translucent circle.
Each time I made it out a little further
before a crack told I had gone too far
and must patch with a tap of iced water
the slit she said no one could see
though the line worried us both.
Once I took her out to the ends of the pastry cloth—
But the thing tore! We laughed,
for I had explored my dough and got
three shells and some left over
to lattice the top of the cherry tart.
We did our best baking on late afternoons,
the light falling like glaze on the cabinets,
the pin clacking as she rolled out pastry enough
for eclairs, Napoleons, cream puffs,
while all I could do was pie shells.
By evening we had rolled, crimped,
sealed and jaggered everything!
The pies browned, the pastries puckered
in the cavernous oven I waited to open.
An aroma, thick as a bite, made my head light.
Gloved with two pot holders, I listened
while she told how not long ago
a girl could not marry until she could roll
her dough so transparent her beloved
could read his Bible through it.
I dreamed of stretching my pastry dough out
to cover the earth with a crust so fine

my love would think it was nothing
but the world at his feet,
baked by the summer sun,
dusted with cinnamon.

What Could It Be?

Around the kettle of chicken and rice,
the aunts were debating what flavor was missing.
Tía Carmen guessed garlic.
Tía Rosa, some coarsely ground pepper.
Tía Ana, so tidy she wore the apron,
shook her head, plain salt what was needed.
Tía Fofi, afraid to be wrong, echoed salt.
Just a pinch, she apologized, and reached for the shaker.
Tía Gladys said parsley never hurt anything.
Tía Victoria frowned and pronounced,
Tarragon. No one disagreed.

The tarragon dotted the rice in the cauldron.
And now, as if signaled, the spice jars popped open,
unloading their far eastern wonders:
cumin, turmeric, saffron, and endives.
The aunts each put in a shake of their favorites.
The steam unwrinkled the frowns from their faces.
They cackled like witches, sampled, and nodded.

Around the table the uncles were grunting,
wolfing their food down, gnawing their chicken bones.
And yet the aunts stopped in the middle of swallows,
heads cocked at each other as if they had heard
in some far off room their own baby crying.
It needed a pinch more of . . . saffron? Paprika?
What could it be they had missed putting in?
The uncles ate seconds and rose in a chorus
of chair scrapes and belches,
falling to slumber on living room couches,
empty plates glowed like the eyes of the spellbound.

Posture Lesson

Mother caught us bending at the waist to brush
dust in a dustpan or unthread a thread
from the rug, legs braced, knees locked. She scolded
the damage we had done the tibia
or femur or pelvis or vertebra.
She had picked up from my father's practice
the names of some bones and could predict ugly
consequences for the wrong moves we made:
pigeon toes, knock knees, hunchback, or the worst,
curvature of the spine. She lined us up
against the wall and tried to worm her hand
behind us, barking orders at our caved-in
chests and doubled chins. *Imagine*, she said,
I've decorated you with epaulets
that weigh your shoulders down. Pretend I've set
a saucer on your head—my good china
you mustn't drop—and walk as if I'd chalked
a line to that wall. We stiffened and set off,
afraid of x-rays at father's office
and fittings for back braces at prom time.
Her inspection dragged on. Out came the tape.
Our hips and busts were inches off the chart:
we were five feet but misfitted with waists
the size for five foot fives. *It's important*
for girls to know how to carry themselves,
she coached, showing us how to sit up straight
so if she dropped a pebble through our crowns,
it'd fall in the great bowl of the pelvis.
She taught us how to walk as if a cord
tied to our heads drew us, gently, skyward.
We tried to stand equal to that summons,

holding our breaths for momentary
pretty silhouettes....
               Then back to our housework,
we hunched over our ironing or bunched
in froggy squats beside our soapy buckets,
backs buckling, all elbows and buttocks.

New Clothes

I remember her on rainy days making my school clothes,
gathering the skirt, pinning the belt to the upside-down waist.
Always reverse, work on the blind. She lifted the lining,
pins in her mouth, words minced between tight lips.
Flip it over and see, the work doesn't show, blind stitches.
She smiled: puckered sleeves, tucked yokes,
lace binding on every seam:
her craft more perfect in invisibility,
her outfits successes when they looked
as if she hadn't made them.

I remember the whirr and whine of her black Singer,
the gold traceries on the cast-iron rod
by the wheel that lifted and lowered the needle.
Threading the levers, eyepieces, winding the turquoise string
through hooks, around miniscule wheels, up and down,
her Ariadne hands were clever in labyrinths,
the fabric rounding and flattening as it neared the flatbed,
the bulb dotting the cloth with a spot of light,
the needle racing through gingham, poplin, seersucker, cambric,
the pedal pressed heavily down with weight of one woman,
eye intent, hands feeding and receiving the fabric.

Sometimes she let me stand on her left side,
taking the fabric in hand as it came through the portal.
Don't tug. Don't hurry it, she snapped. *Thread'll snag.*
Minute by minute, patient impatience, shifting from foot to foot,
I begged for the odd job:
taking a seam out, sewing a hem, snipping off thread ends.

Sometimes she let me stand on her right side,
turning the wheel slowly by hand till she pinched, *Stop!*

Handing her scissors by handle-ears, *Never the sharp end, never!*
threading her needles, winding her threads;
the spools sat in their rods in the sewing box,
ends tucked in the notch on the flat tops,
a palette of greens, laurel, mint, olive, aquamarine,
shorts, skirts, blouses, dresses, and nightgowns—
better than storebought.

Late in the night she worked, bent, peering at stitches.
I stayed up, dabbing her seams with a damp facecloth,
pressing the wet hiss out of my dresses.
Sometimes she stopped, turning back over a seam,
forward and back, reinforcement, then snip.
She held out the bell of a skeletal skirt for me to try,
rubbed at the small of her back, glanced at the time.
Oh my! It's late. Tomorrow's a schoolday!
She rushed me upstairs, hurried a facewash,
turned my arms into the sleeves of the nightgown she'd made me,
tucked me between sheets that smelled of her handcream.

I waited in the dark she left me
for the creak of descent,
the scrape of the chair,
the furious whirr of the Singer.

Naming the Fabrics

Mother, unroll the bolts and name
the fabrics from which our clothing came,
dress the world in vocabulary:
broadcloth, corduroy, denim, terry,

gingham and calico, crepe and gauze,
gabardine, organdy, wool, madras—
fabrics, Mother, name them all,
jersey, chambray, satin, voile.

*

the mother speaks

Give me a yard of that dotted swiss,
satin to rein in my junior miss
with a crimson sash and a show-off bow,
for school clothes yards of that calico.

Of course I'd like some permanent press,
with four daughters and a man to dress!
I've got them down to a set of numbers
though the girls keep inching out of their jumpers.

I'd like a lick of that wedge of velvet,
rich as a bar of chocolate fudge.
My husband blames that sheer chiffon
for our four girls he sowed as sons.

All the better! Four sets of hands
to puzzle the squares on a yard of lawn,
outline in chalk, then satin-stitch
the monograms on his handkerchiefs.

I pay a tailor to cut his suits
from seersucker, duck, tweed, cheviot,
those names make my cutting hand skittish—
either they sound like sex or British.

My girls were cut out of different cloths,
my legs scissoring with love
(they're old enough to hear it said)
on the muslin sheets of my homemade bed.

My eldest is jersey, a sensible fabric,
to make up for my second, a pretty dramatic
damask. The third is genuine kersey.
My baby, a finicky dimity.

As for me, if I had to pick,
I'd be a reversible fabric,
on the worn-out side, a wife and mother,
a brand-new woman on the other

with wash-and-wear marquisette legs and feet,
organdy thighs, a thin tricot waist,
a chambray bodice and brocade breasts,
wrinkle-free orlon on my face.

*

Mother, you'll last in marquisette,
brocade, chambray. For when your spirit
discards itself from the spindle spine,
we'll hang your clothes on the washday line.

And the sleeves will fill with windy limbs,
the busts bulge with a sudden gust,
the hips indulge in the fattening wind,
and the snap of the breeze be the thump of the pulse.

Four sets of hands will tend to you.
For although your being has fallen through
the weave of these fabrics, still you live
as the damp lap dries and the tight seams give

in the gingham, calico, crepe, and gauze,
gabardine, organdy, wool, madras—
fabrics, Mother, you've known them all,
jersey, chambray, satin, voile.

Orchids

I

Oh, she would never marry,
my maiden aunt, Tía Chica!
They gave her run of the garden.
She grew bougainvillea on a trellis;
her anthuriums by the driveway
had cups as big as my palms,
pistils aimed at the sky.
Her rock garden inclined
up towards a stone Saint Francis,
a birdbath in his arms,
rude droppings on his shoulders.
On his tonsure perched a sparrow,
preening his fussy feathers.
The guava trees and tamarinds
lined the cool path to the shack
I was not allowed to enter.
I'd climb for what seemed the blush
of pink on a ripe guava,
but the wormy ones I found
were never worth the bother.
Down I'd come to the shady,
forbidden edge of the garden.

They said she would never marry!
She had done well enough by her father.
(He gave her run of the garden.)
Besides, what man would put up
with a lady who was so bossy?
Her eye didn't miss a tendril!

She wore a dress with an apron
made of a flowered fabric,
her little garden gloves
flew in and out of the foliage,
a pearl button at the wrist—
she was always losing the button.
"Come help me with this," she chirped.
My hands cupped her hibiscus
as she gently dusted the stigma
with the pollen of the pistil.
Or she bent a blossom over
and asked me to smell the ginger.

I followed far behind her,
holding her handpicked flowers,
afraid that her giant ferns
would unravel their rolled-up fronds
and grab me when she wasn't looking.
Oh, but she punished the fresh ones
with a snip of her garden scissors!

But never was I allowed
to help her with her rare orchids
in that little slatted shack
at the edge of her father's garden.

The men of the Orchid Society
came with rulers, thermometers,
little notebooks scribbled with numbers.
She escorted them down the path,
behind the hedge of hibiscus,
half shaded by the guavas,
to the little slatted shack
I was not allowed to enter.
The men came back astonished,

wiping their creased foreheads:
"Twenty-two varieties!
The work of a single woman?"

Once I sneaked to the edge of the garden,
pushed back the wicker gate.
(Those hinges were tattletales.)
My mouth dropped at the vision:
her orchids, her orchids. . . .
An arching spray of tongues
hung from a swaying cradle,
scarlet and faint lavender,
pink mouths breathed at my ear,
slippers and little purses,
purple, spotted spiders . . .
their gooey lips, their stickiness,
the pouches slightly distended,
seemed intimate and forbidden.
I heard the trickle of water
from a hose outside in the garden
and swayed drunk with the scent
from a row of perfumed trumpets.
Shaken, I backed out
from the shack in her father's garden.

II

In her thirties she married well,
a lawyer in New York City.
They lived neighbors to the sky
in the penthouse of a high rise.
She grew geraniums and lilies
and a poinsettia in season.
Her little boy played Brahms
every summer by the window.

She invited me for late lunches
during my school vacations.
She remembered, she said, the orchids,
they were a good diversion,
though twenty-two varieties
were hard work for a single woman!

I asked her to name the orchids.
"Let's see," she said as she sipped
the espresso she had made us
from a tiny porcelain cup
that seemed borrowed from a child.

First there were the Brassias,
commonly known as Spiders;
the easiest were the Vandas;
the Epidendrums were show-offs.
Oncidiums and Mormodes,
just too many to remember.
Jewel Box and Queerie Deeries,
impudent little faces!
White Nuns and Lady Slippers,
and her prize, the very rare
fluttery white Diacrum
still feared by the orchid hunters,
who claimed the flowers had stingers.
The secret was, she whispered,
fire ants lived in the pouches!
They had bitten her here and there.
But the arm she held out to show me
was as smooth as her white Diacrum.

III

Oh, the children must be raised,
the piano cover lifted,
the metronome beat seconded
with the nods of a proud mother.
The husband too has his stories
and needs the "ah" of a listener
who has never heard such wonders.
The grandfather must be wiped
when he dribbles like a newborn.
But I celebrate for a moment
the single-minded labors
of the single woman artist:
the widow squeezes the whey
through the cheesecloth that she bunches,
the shy nuns stitch their crosses
on the linens of the altar,
the silly lacemakers knot
a thousand complications
as they giggle and they gossip.
And Tía Chica bred twenty-two
varieties of orchids.

I name them in celebration:
Brassias and Dendrobiums,
Epidendrums and Vandas,
Oncidiums and Mormodes,
Jewel Box and Queerie Deeries,
White Nuns and Lady Slippers,
and her prize the very rare
fluttery white Diacrum.
Twenty-two varieties
bred by a single woman!

Charges

I used to clean her patio for free
until my cousin told me he got paid
a quarter by his mother for the job.
So I wrote up a schedule of my fees:
a dime for dusting, a nickel to sweep
the yard, a dollar to do the whole house.

Next time she needed something in the house,
I gave her the menu and said, feel free
to combine jobs, for instance, I could sweep
and mop the hall, she'd only have to pay
for one, and I'd negotiate a fee
if she thought I charged too high for a job.

You should have seen her face—it was a job
to look at her. I looked around the house:
All the little price tags I'd set as fees
for different jobs went blank. "I'll work for free,"
I offered, but it was too late. I paid
the consequence for weeks for getting swept

away by my cousin's making a clean sweep
over at his place. Anytime a job
came up, she went at it herself and paid
no attention when I begged to clean house
as a favor to *me*. Her love flowed free
only when I tore up that list of fees.

To this day when I have to charge a fee
·I apologize and tactfully sweep
the bills in my purse or do it for free
rather than say there's a charge for the job.
I always feel the whole world is her house!
I always see her face when I get paid

as if I'm not worthy of the payment!
I've come to see my guilt as memory's fee
for recalling that first time that her house
became a market for her love. I've swept
her rejection away as if my job
were to maintain her love for me dirt-free.

But she could have paid me pennies to clean house.
Her love should have been free, not swept away
as a fee for the hard job of being my mother.

Mother Love

I tell you not to trust a man with that,
my mother warned as I tucked in my side,
only a mother's love does not go bad.

We made the beds—she gave her side a pat
as if to check no one was tucked inside.
How could she trust a girl to stay intact,

a girl who let her beaten eggs fall flat,
and soaked (in bleach) her coloreds with her whites?
Those stains, she said, were future loves gone bad.

She beat her eggs into a foamy wrath,
listing the sins that she would not abide.
I swore to her I'd not do things like that!

She roared her vacuum over the welcome mat
to vanish those she didn't want inside.
She knew by looking whose love would go bad.

The house gleamed clean as if it'd been ransacked
of all the fantasies which she denied.
I broke my oath—trusting a man with that—
and found only her mother love went bad.

Woman's Work

Who says a woman's work isn't high art?
She challenged as she scrubbed the bathroom tiles.
Keep house as if the address were your heart.

We cleaned the whole upstairs before we started
downstairs. I sighed, hearing my friends outside.
Doing her woman's work was a hard art

to practice when the summer sun would bar
the floor I swept till she was satisfied.
She kept me prisoner in her housebound heart.

She shined the tines of forks, the wheels of carts,
cut lacy lattices for all her pies.
Her woman's work was nothing less than art.

And I, her masterpiece since I was smart,
was primed, praised, polished, scolded, and advised
to keep a house much better than my heart.

I did not want to be her counterpart!
I struck out ... but became my mother's child:
a woman working at home on her art,
housekeeping paper as if it were her heart.

for Judy Yarnall

HEROINES

Heroines

We keep coming to this part
of the story where we're sad.
I've broken up with my true love
man after man.
You've found It.
Once, It was God.
Once, revolution
in the third world.
Now, It's love.

You'll survive, our mothers said
when romance was once.
Now they keep tight faces
for our visits home
and tell their friends
all that education
has confused us,
all those poems.

They have, we laugh,
and buy the dreams—
*Redbook, House Beautiful,
Mademoiselle*, and *Vogue*—
to read our stories in them
and send the clippings home.
Sometimes the bright chase
of lovers in a meadow
sets us to believe again
in the worn plot of love.

Sadly, we turn the page
to right our hearts,
knowing our lives too well
to be the heroines
of our mothers' stories.
We're careful with the words
we pick, the loves with no returns
like the ones we wanted.
Godmothers to our sisters' girls,
we bring them squawking rubber monsters,
birthday poems pasted in the growing albums.

for C.

Woman Friend

Before you round the corner and are gone
I wave and note how easily my palm
blots out your car, the motor's hum
merges with Sunday traffic back from church.
You drove up for a weekend visit
to give my life a closer reading,
then catch me up on your story:
both plots, this time, going well,
the heroines about to make big moves
we hope will end with love.

If not, that's what we're friends for.
late nights or weekends when the rates
go down, we call and splurge on sadness,
bad dreams, or good intentions that become
ambivalent in deed, desires to be saved
in some big way we've learned about in the movies.
Always, we bring up love, either in its past tense
as loss or in its future, longing.
Afraid of weekend loneliness, we meet
and call it since we're women, *friends*.

Before you left, we hugged, promised absolutes
we hope we won't be called to account for
midweek when we're hard at work
earning the living husbands used to pay for
when we were heroines of our mothers' stories.
After you leave, I clean house, fold your bedding,
roll the mattress back into the couch
and tidy any little disorder you created
by being here. Ashamed, I've saved my heart-
breaks for the men who come and go.

Wallpaper

He said in his mother's house, growing up
he remembered roses, and his friend said
his mother could not abide print on her walls,
whether determined children swinging their swing ropes taut,
or tidy cottages, their chimney smoke trained upwards.
She wanted no pretense of happiness, the rooms gift-wrapped
with trotting horses or teakettles pouring.
She could not abide them and tore off, sanded,
painted blank the little dogs barking,
ladies with umbrella and muff.

His companion remembered his mother on a stepladder,
rolling out roses, hundreds of roses, thousands,
since she papered not just the halls and the living room
but the kitchen alcove where he and she sat
eating meal after meal after his father left
and she relied solely on him for company,
for belief in *something* in her fury and grief.
Still she insisted they live in this perpetual celebration
of rose petals, which grew vague with repetition,
vague with his vivid daydreams of running away.

We were standing all three at a party
and since I could not tell yet
whether these two men were paired together
or paired only in their interest of me,
I was listening, carefully, leaning back against the wall
like Vuillard's sister in the painting of his mother and sister,
the print of her dress the same pattern as the wallpaper,
so that she is disappearing into the wall, as I was,
the better to listen for who these men might be
by what they were saying of their mothers.

Against Cinderella

Whoever made it up is pulling my foot
so it'll fit that shoe.
I'll go along with martyrdom—
she swept and wept, mended, stoked the fire,
slaved while her three stepsisters,
who just happened to oblige their meanness
by being ugly, dressed themselves.
I'll swallow that there was a Singer godmother
who magically could sew a pattern up
and hem it in an hour,
that Cinderella got to be a debutante
and lost her head and later lost her shoe.
But there I stop.
I can't believe only one woman in that town
had that size foot, could fit into that shoe.
I've felt enough of lost and found
to know that if you lose your heart
to anyone you've crowned into a prince,
you might not get it back.
That the old kerchief trick,
whether you drop a shoe, your clothes, your life,
doesn't do much but litter up the world.
That when the knock at last comes to your door,
you might not be home or willing.
That some of us have learned to go barefoot
knowing the mate to one foot is the other.

Old Heroines

Where do heroines go when their novels are over?
If she's not married off, she gets on a train
and rides to the city to see her old lover—
though it's clear from the ending he has broken things off.
And as she is racing through Russia or Iowa
she looks out the window, the dark fields rolling by,
or maybe the night sky grainy with stars....
She sees her reflection, a face still dramatic,
pale and young in that afterward light.
She wonders, how long must I still play this part?

Outside in those farmhouses bathed in pale porchlight,
the unstoried women who formed the mere backdrop
to her beauty, betrayals, drift off to sleep
in the arms of their husbands, dreaming themselves
in elegant furs racing towards Moscow, Chicago,
some heady excitement! They wake with a start,
turning on lights to make sure of their status—
brief lights she beholds from her jailhouse train
as she rides on forever in the haze of bright dreams
which her sorrows inspire in these happier women.

33

33

Everything that happens to me these days
is dangerous with love. I'm a witch
at full moon. I can't be sure
of anyone. I stiffen if I'm grazed
by an arm or a hand combs through my hair.
I won't drink from a strange cup or use
borrowed clothing. Everything is infused
with hazard and imagination's power,
stronger than actual. I won't accept
dinner invitations in case magic
powders have been disguised in the garlic
seasonings. But my house, though protected
with charms, can't block the spell mortality
has cast, thirty-two, I turn thirty-three.

I got divorced at twenty-nine and vowed
I'd put the energy I used for love
in some constructive cause. I thought of how
Emily, Mother Teresa, Joan of Arc
had given themselves to more than romance.
I too could write or save far eastern towns
or starving kids. I went unsexed for months,
recorded dreams in journals, joined the Friends
for weekly pacificism, I even
adopted a Latin American
girl orphan over the mail, cheap, and when
men came on to me, I said, Let's be friends.
But if they fell in love with other women,
I felt unfeminist and feminine.

Mami asks what I'm up to, that means men
in any declension except sex; it
means do I realize I am thirty-
three without a husband, house, or children
and going on thirty-four? Papi extends
an invitation to come live with them,
there are two empty bedrooms I can write
in and handouts until I make it big
which means men at publication parties
asking me what mentors shaped my style
and has anyone told me how beautiful
I am having written something worthwhile?
Their drinks tinkle in their hands like keys
to doors closed at the closing of stories.

My friend Carol says aging evens out
the advantage of beautiful women
over plain ones. The beautiful have to
watch their beauty fade in their own and men's
eyes. I can only talk small, having been
pretty, on good days almost beautiful.
These days in conversation with a man,
I'll catch his eyes searching for beautiful
women in the room, and I want to cry
out: If I could take some years off with my
clothes, you'd find a nice-looking girl before
you! Ex-gorgeous Carol says men ignore
her much more than she's used to or seem bored
with her theories. But I hear you, Carol.

Where are the girls who were so beautiful?
I don't mean back in the olden days either,
I mean yesterday and the day before
yesterday? Tell me, if you can, where will
I find breathless Vivien or Marilyn,
her skirt blown up? Certainly Natalie,
struggling in the cold waves, deserved to be
fished out when the crew finished and given
her monogrammed beach towel and a hot drink.
How many times didn't we pay good money
to see them saved from worse catastrophes
as they trembled in swimsuits on the brink
of death, Rita and Jean, Lana and Joan,
Frances, Marlene—their names sound like our own.

The women on my mother's side were known
for beauty and were given lovely names
passed down for generations. I knew them
as my pretty aunts: Laura, who could turn
any head once, and Ada, whose husband
was so devoted he would lay his hand-
kerchief on seats for her and when she rose
thank her; there was Rosa, who got divorced
twice, her dark eyes and thick hair were to blame;
and my mother, Julia, who was a catch
and looks it in her wedding photographs.
My sister got her looks, I got her name,
and it suits me that between resemblance
and words, I got the right inheritance.

I met a man at a self-improvement
weekend. Most people who were there were sad,
divorced and sad, or in bad marriages
they couldn't leave for convincing arguments
they sadly told about. When his turn came,
he said right out, I want to sleep with you
and touched my hand. The leaders of the group
invited me to share whatever came
into my head. The sad participants
waited; his sad eyes wouldn't let me go.
My sad ex came to mind. He said he hadn't
meant for us to go bad, he loved me so.
Couldn't we try once more? I looked the man
straight in the eyes and sadly answered both.

A man invited me to eat with him
at the Sirloin Saloon. I accepted
although I'm borderline vegetarian
and conversation was all I wanted,
don't ask me why. I said, I know I'm not
supposed to come unless in the back of
my mind I think maybe we've got a lot
in common and could maybe fall in love.
Of course, that's the prime cut! Most likely we're
both starved for sex and split up when we get
too serious. We gabbed till our order
cooled down. It was a pleasure to have met
a woman he could just talk to, he said.
My steak was raw. I cut it and it bled.

Greg's got custody of Sally and wants
to fall in love with a stepmother so
Sally can have a mommie like her friends
in day care and draw two big sticks hold-
ing a little stick with a happy face
between them. They come over to my place,
Sally sits on Dad's lap and sucks her thumb,
hungrily or sadly, we ask which one?
She doesn't know the words for what she feels
yet, so she shrugs her answer: *Don't worry,
I'm okay*. We play Alphabet. Greg says,
A, and I answer, *Apple*. Sally laughs,
unstoppering her mouth. We have a ways
before we get to the letter for *love*.

In my dream I was a closet mermaid,
my tail tucked in my jeans, a long braid
down my back. I was supposedly
in love, but his neediness had turned me
off, though it was also a seductive bond.
I'd gone off to a wild party, alone,
and was having intense yet casual fun
with a half dozen men. Somehow I found
out he was downstairs asking where I was—
the good dream suddenly turned bad. I asked
the guys to please excuse me for a sec,
went down, gabbed with him, used the same pretext
to go upstairs, but felt his pull again.
I, one, he, another kind of siren.

I ask a married friend about a man.
Listen, she says, pretend, and in the end,
you're not able to tell the difference
between the real and the induced romance.
Remember Hamlet tells his wayward mom,
"Assume a virtue if you haven't one,
the next night will be easier to be good"?
Whether this man was meant to be your true
and everlasting love's beside the point.
After a time all lovers disappoint
their loves, that's when a marriage starts!
And then, his well-off, considerate, good heart
will keep you happier much longer than
some true love you mistook for a husband.

Tell me what is it women want the most?
Is it what most everyone says, a man,
a rich, kind, liberated man
who figures out what we want? Be honest
now, whatever our public politics,
is that it? Or do we most want power
over our men as I read in Chaucer—
the tables turned and set for *us* to eat?
Or is it kids? Biology being
thicker than history, each feminist
a repressed mother who'd be happiest
with a family? Or are we fooling
ourselves when we know what we want is love—
the problem is no one to ask it of.

My gay friends ask, Well are you gay or what?
And men agree we're friends, but don't I want
a man? Or husband, my mother wonders,
Don't you want children? My sister wishes
I'd end up with a man who also wants
to change the world and is willing to work
for it. The two of you could do peace work
and stuff, she says, certainly you'd worry
less if you were having more sex. It's weird
not to be with someone, man or woman,
even a nun though celibate is wed
to Jesus Christ. What kind of a woman
are you? I wish I knew, I say, I wish
I knew and could just put it into words.

33 is the year that Jesus Christ
took the big leap, the minister teases.
I've come to take the edge off loneliness
by being convinced that maybe god exists,
is with me in the empty bed, with me
when I can't do up the back of my dress,
with me for bread and cheese since recipes
depress me with leftovers, and just is.
Wasn't he crucified at 33,
I ask, depressed, deserted by his friends,
divorced from god, subject to human laws?
Wasn't he the most single finally
at 33, meeting his lonely end?
Yes, the minister takes my hand, he was.

Are we all ill with acute loneliness,
chronic patients trying to recover
the will to love? Yet all we've suffered
from others and ourselves, all the losses
of faith in the human face—when we glimpsed
the animal in the mother's grimace
or in the lover's grin as he promised
the promise no one can keep—made us lapse
back into our separateness. We all feel
absence like a wound. Sometimes the love
of another wounded one acts like a salve
which soothes the dying self but cannot heal
our lives. And perhaps this is what it feels
like to be human, and we are all well?

Let's make a modern primer for our kids:
A is for Auschwitz; B for Biafra;
Chile; Dachau; El Salvador; F is
the Falklands; Grenada; Hiroshima
stands for H; Northern Ireland for I;
J is for Jonestown; K for Korea;
L for massacres in Lidice; My Lai;
N, Nicaragua; O, Okinawa;
P is the Persian Gulf and Qatar, Q;
Rwanda; Sarajevo—this year's hell;
T is Treblinka and Uganda U;
Vietnam and Wounded Knee. What's left to spell?
An X to name the countless disappeared
when they are dust in Yemen or Zaire.

Posit our little stays against the mad
possibilities of being human:
against Hiroshima, let's play Handel's
Messiah, turned up loud, so that the blast
of trumpets drowns out bombing in Vietnam.
Or let's recite a poem by Yeats, *alto voce*,
until we do not hear the cries at Auschwitz
or Dachau, pit Hitler against Whitman,
a dozen Rembrandts against Genghis Khan.
Who wins? —But these are evil balances,
for any comparison mitigates
brutalities we must leave absolute
so we never, no never, no matter the Homers,
never forgive them, never, never, never.

Or should we forgive them? Auschwitz? Berlin?
For they're dramas genetic to our hearts
and to protest we never played the part
leaves us open to history's rerun
starring us as victim or villain.
Look closely at the evil of the race
in every case it wears a human face,
sometimes our own in inspired proportions.
But should we claim more than biology
for our species? Humans must be humane—
or what? What shall we do with those insane
Nazi brutes who downgrade humanity?
Gas them and declare that to be human
is not to have too much to be forgiven?

My parents are in Germany as guests
of a Gerontology Conference.
Mami mailed the cards so that they'd get
here on or about March 27th.
Today three strangely large envelopes come
with (in her hand) DO NOT OPEN UNTIL
YOUR BIRTHDAY. The first card's a Hallmark poem
about how daughters are incredible.
The second one is meant to make me laugh:
a middle finger tied with a ribbon
(a hint they missed) says, Don't forget to have
a ball, love, Mom, Dad's name written by Mom.
In the last one's a check, the memo reads,
Get yourself something in our name you need.

Get yourself something in our name you need,
Sounds wistful, sounds like they already know
their daughter's life is turbulent, and so
to make up for it, here's pocket money!
Oh God, they think, watching the sad rain fall
from their Munich hotel the afternoon
of my birthday, Why did we bring children
into a world we can't make heads or tails
or sense out of? Perhaps they're visiting
monuments to man's inhumanity
to man, and she turns to him asking simply,
Why? And for comfort they hold hands, wandering
where thousands died. And I want suddenly
to give them something, anything, they need.

And suddenly my name comes to their lips.
Why not call her? my father asks. She smiles
as he picks up the receiver and dials,
and in Vermont a phone rings in my sleep.
I stumble through the house, fumbling my way
in the darkness, on my lips a curse for
whoever woke me, but also terror
some tragedy that wouldn't keep till day
is at the other end to wreck my dreams.
Yeah? I challenge. I hear a faint *Hello* ...
and someone's name I can't make out. *HELLO!*
I shout madly, and hear my father scream,
Hang up, love, the connection is terrible!
I lay my end, gently, in its cradle.

I check my parents' house while they're abroad
during a weekend in New York. I drive
through their exclusive neighborhood, arrive
at dusk, remembering Mami's horror
stories of recent break-ins within blocks.
The door's rigged up with an alarm, three locks,
and inside, an emergency button,
which if I press will make the police come.
The windows are all wired to the alarm
and can't be opened. Despite this, five times
they've gotten in and robbed them clean. Inside
the key box in the hall, I find a sealed
envelope: FOR OUR FOUR DAUGHTERS, OPEN
ONLY IN CASE OF DEATH FOR INSTRUCTIONS.

I hesitate—the box was left unlocked,
the envelope is fat with information.
Inside, most probably, I'll find mention
of funeral arrangements, whom to ask
about the will, which of us four's in charge
of doing what, a list of phone numbers
of who should know. And knowing my mother,
reminders of clothes at the cleaners, yard
work to be done this spring, a vacuum hose
due at Sears. Then money matters, each one
gets her quarter. But I admit I want
more, a private letter that discloses
I'm heir to the largest share of their love.
I hesitate—before I lock the box.

Happy Birthday! Happy Birthday! The calls
are coming in from California, New
York, Massachusetts, long lost childhood
friends remember, a showing of aunts, all
my sisters telephone or write, old lovers
excuse themselves from cozy moments to
call from pay phones, *Happy Birthday to you.*
I sing along, but have to hang up, there's
someone at the door. It's UPS
with two parcels! The delivery guy,
a handsome lad, guesses it's my birthday
and asks how old I am. He acts surprised
he's a decade younger. We linger at the door,
one of us not immortal anymore.

I close my door. Anchored on either side
by a package, I watch him drive away
in his big brown hive of a truck. I sigh,
my sweet bumblebee boy's scared off by age
that doesn't look so bad. At least Cupid
in his brown regimentals has left me
two parcels of his UPS honey.
His truck pulls up again! He's so sorry,
forgot to have me sign where the X is.
We smile a long smile. I sign once, twice,
he says my name over as if misspelled,
then laughs, I laugh, we linger. How the hell
do you end something like this, I wonder?
SHE: (wistfully) If I were ten years younger....

HE: Age doesn't matter when you're both in love!
SHE: You say that now, wait till you've had enough.
HE: I love for keeps. I'll never let you down.
SHE: You lie, my dear, you'll lay me in the ground.
HE: Statistics say I'll probably die first.
SHE: Statistics say most couples get divorced.
HE: Better to love and lose than not at all.
SHE: Better to read the writing on the wall!
HE: You go by loss, you might as well not live.
SHE: Or live, single, and psychoanalyzed.
HE: It breaks my heart to hear you talk that way.
SHE: (boy in her arms, wiping his tears away,
prescribes the cure for existential ache)
Come in, my sweet, and have some birthday cake.

Hey, I say to the UPS boy,
I've got some birthday cake, some soda pop.
How about a break? He smiles, but says
he'd better not, he's not allowed to stop
on his route, boss checks up on him, one guy
lost his job for helping a nice lady
screw in a bulb. I shake my head (sadly)
over that one. Encouraged, he tells me
believe-it-or-not stories of his boss,
clips and unclips his clipboard to remind
us both he'd better go ... but one more loss
of faith renews his stay. My only lines
now are, *You're kidding me!* or *Jesus Christ!*
Lady, he says as he leaves, you're real nice.

Sometimes I'll fall in love with the wrong man
because I want the valentine movie
so much I'll play it with whoever leads,
I don't care who since I never see him
anyhow for all my projections on
his John Doe face. A couple of times I've
wondered if he's all there is to love,
and love's hard work is turning visions off,
adjusting my sights to a real person,
who's in turn trying to be genuine
in spite of romance programs he was taught,
both of us waiting till the movie stops
to learn to love. Sometimes I think it's him
squirming in his seat, too, bored with this film!

I'm watching a romantic movie play
in Plato's cave; half of the time I don't
believe in it and put the management
down for its taste. Take that crap off! I say.
Other times I get so addicted, I'm
one of the mainliners, high on romance,
hallucinating that in truth a man's
body is one of the Absolute Forms.
I look around when the houselights come on
and see . . . no one! I wonder if they've gone
out in the sunlight for enlightenment,
each half with its matched other, holding hands,
while punished for my doubts, I'm tantalized
with movies of what's going on outside.

The evil eye, a look more common than
you think, a daily way we see the world
colored by what we need so that the world
is a movie for our entertainment
and strangers we marry or give birth to
are villains or best friends of the hero
in the film we project of our ego's
Perilous Journey. Someone who sees you
with too much emotion cannot see you,
and that, more than hocus-pocus, is what
it means to cast an evil eye. I'm not
one to talk since lately I don't seem to—
except in writing—take anyone to heart
and love them in person. Lie there, my art.

Why do we love one man, not another?
Seems like the heart is a child who ignores
an expensive gift so as to explore
the box it came in. We fall for trifles.
For Bruce because when his marriage broke up,
he counted all the steps to his new house
with his daughter and felt relieved it was
a number she could count to without help.
For Jamie because the week he visited,
he carved me a whole set of Plato's forms
in wood: a square, globe, cube, pyramid, cone.
His last night we picked favorites, then he used
the globe to prop my bedroom window open
because it was the one I had chosen.

For Gordon because he wasn't ashamed
to say he loved his wife, unlike husbands
who tell their mistresses they stay married
with the mothers because of the children.
For Clive because that morning at the Tate
looking at Turners, his eyes wet before
those luminous canvases of ships moored
in light, wondered aloud what it would take
to keep me in London, and suddenly,
before I could say *love*, my heart flooded
with light. I saw on Clive's face all
losses past and to come, Julian, Jamie,
Gordon, Steven, Bruce, John. I embraced Clive
because it was too late to stop myself.

There we were at the Tate before Turner's
Ships at Sea in hot embrace. Tourists passed
smiling, even the guards grinned, no one asked
us to move apart so they could see Turner's
Ships at Sea. I thought, if there was thinking
going on inside my head, Clive, let's get
out or we're going to be on the carpet
in a minute. The ships at sea sailed on.
The tourists boarded their buses. London
traffic cymbaled and clanged as we clung on
to what there was of Other that wasn't
Us, waves of lust rocked us, the honeyed sun
fell in sweet streams through the seablue skylights. . . .
We spent a week in love, promised to write
as I boarded. The plane climbed into light.

Clive, who are you with these days? The mailograms
tied with a rubber band are in a box
in my parents' garage. Or Julian,
has your new true love bothered you with lots
of questions about how we were? Tell her
everything. Don't spare her with softened truths
the hard loving we did. Tell her lovers
always bring their ghostly crew of past loves,
and by our age our beds are so crowded
they feel like arks in which all those we've loved
are set adrift with us. We lay our heads
where another forehead lay. It touches me
to touch so many persons in one,
which is why love does for religion.

Ever have an older lover say: God!
I once thought I used to love so and so
so much, but now that I love you, I know
that wasn't love. Even though it feels good
at our age to be flattered with being
the first woman a man has ever loved,
it burns my blood thinking of those I loved
with my whole soul (small as it was back then)
quibble if what they felt for me was love
now that they've had a taste of the real stuff.
I say, Don't trust those men with better,
bigger versions of love if they refuse
the small, shabby sample they gave others
the tribute of believing it was true.

Given the choice, whom would I choose to love?
There have been times I always chose a man;
now, if anything, I shy from romance
so other loves can have a chance to thrive.
I'm in love with multitudes: schoolteachers
dispensing stars, sons with their big workhands
clapped on their fathers' shoulders, white-haired friends
comparing childhoods, workers whose hoarse
voices shout above their machines, writers
reading each other favorite passages
from a book, or briefer marriages,
times when I speak from the heart to strangers
I trust, times when I know that each single
blessed thing is eligible for love.

I was driving down the mountain, the curves
were bad, I wasn't going slow, the day
was one of those that takes your breath away:
a late summer sky so blue it hurts
to look at it too long encouraged faith.
On hilltops, I made believe I'd take off
into that absolute, but as I swerved
again and again from the edge and hugged
the double center line, and as the sun's
autumnal, soporific light shone on
the glinting roofs and church steeple below,
something gave in me ... and I let it go—
this driving need to make it all mean more.
In time, I turned the wheel back to the road.

I was driving down the mountain, I had
a job starting in a month, but nothing
before that certainty, a gap I find
I slip through if not careful and go mad.
I hadn't been careful, I'd been reckless
at a mountaintop writers' conference,
drinking too much, staying up until late,
pretending to more passion or talent
than I have. My midnight revelations
were embarrassing to flashback on
during workshops the next morning in which
writers whose bestsellers had made them rich
warned us against giving our characters
our own predictable, excessive lives.

Driving down the mountain, flashbacking on
driving up the mountain ten days before
at the start of the conference, the car
packed hurriedly with everything I owned.
I had just quit my job, left my husband,
said goodbye to my friends, and driven east
six days on interstate, without the least
idea what I'd do in ten days when
the conference ended. My manuscript
of stories lay beside me, the station
blared the blues, and as I reached the summit,
that spot renowned for sacrifice and vision,
I wondered what else I had to offer
besides my own excessive character?

The critic was kind. He quoted Auden,
offered me, midmorning, a glass of wine,
and complimented here and there a line
as memorable. I saw marks on the margin
that looked crueler than his remarks out loud,
question marks or whole paragraphs crossed out,
heroes scolded for giving in to plot
or heroines sent back to be described.
I tried to listen, take notes, kindly
not finishing his quotes, and stared out
on a New England meadow straight from Frost:
acres of grasses and flowers tossed by
a wind which whirled with the continual
roar of a thousand voices at Babel.

Driving down the mountain, all stays
against madness had fallen away.
The guardrail was crumpled round a curve
where someone drunk or desperate had swerved
at the last minute and saved herself for . . .
for the Edenic-looking towns below.
I kept myself back with the names of towns
and car makes, headed for friends in Boston,
not knowing if the vowels and consonants
could stay the insubstantial pageant.
I murmured Nova, Stockbridge, Royalton,
Escort, White River Junction, Lebanon,
Honda, Saab. . . . The words rose up like buildings
and, slowly, defined the Boston skyline.

In Boston lived my friends Ken and Carol,
my sister Maury, more names to stay me
with their clean consonants and vowels.
I felt consoled their streets were named for trees,
Elmwood and Maple, Birch, reminding me
of woods I'd just been in, which called to mind
the wildflowers I'd seen, asters, daisies,
and queen anne's lace, and that brought on the names
of girlfriends who had gone to school with me
and still lived in Boston, Laurel, Heather,
with children, Tommie, Laurie, and husbands,
Tom and Jason. By month's end I was happier,
settled, working, writing—in a word, *cured*.
Madness was just another, dirty word.

I was sitting at my desk this morning
trying to get a poem I was having
trouble with in an umpteenth revision
over and done with, but by this version
what I had written wasn't what I meant
but sounded hollow and self-important.
When right below my window in their drive,
the next door lovers were saying goodbye.
She, in her nightgown, clung to him, her cries
muffled for her mouth was pressed where his heart
should be. He, dressed to go, pried her away,
but relenting, held her. Then his gaze strayed
to me, writing, and he raised his eyebrows
as if we were fellow conspirators.

Perhaps I do have a lot in common
with my next-door Romeo whom I've cast
as a two-faced, behind-the-back Don Juan,
wanting to get as close as he can get
to Juliet and Helen and Iseult
and recent vintages of the above.
I've always liked the gaiety of lust
combined with the committed heart of love.
Yet I've backed off from both, afraid I'd get
the balance wrong or be told I presume
too much. I've tried my moves out here instead,
getting as close as I can in this poem,
and now, closer. There's nothing you can do.
By now, I am already inside you.

Secretly I am building in the heart
a delicate structure like one of those
cardhouses or Popsicle palaces
kids build, patiently piecing each part
together, fingers pinching a small tube
of glue, eyes straining to perceive what new
thing I am making that takes so much time
to finish if there's finish in these things.
And making it out of nothing but what
are ruins from an earlier effort
and tempted constantly to believe that
a readymade is better, and yet I've
labored with my heart to outlast the heart
with this thing I'm creating out of love.

Sometimes the words are so close I am
more who I am when I'm down on paper
than anywhere else as if my life were
practising for the real me I become
unbuttoned from the anecdotal and
unnecessary and undressed down
to the figure of the poem, line by line,
the real text a child could understand.
Why do I get confused living it through?
Those of you lost and yearning to be free,
who hear these words, take heart from me.
I once was in as many drafts as you.
But briefly, essentially, here I am.
Who touches this poem touches a woman.

REDWING
SONNETS

Redwing Sonnets

He's carrying on with a distracting song
this early morning while I'm revising
a poem I've tried for years to make as strong
as I'm able. I think he's a redwing
blackbird—but I'm not sure—not having learned
the little lore that comes from staying put
long enough in a place to hear birdsong
or to know what that whatchamacallit
with a hanging thingamajig is called.
I tell you, I think half the fun (or more)
of being alive in the world is learning
the names of things so there are no *things* at all
left in the world, so that dying you know
exactly what you are leaving behind.

*

Which is why I've stuck with this old poem
I mentioned, that treats an awful period
in my life when I fell for the wrong men,
had a score of phobias that ran riot
over my common sense and a closet
I could barely close for all the skeletons
I didn't want to name or know about.
Now that I'm happy I should sink those bones
deep in a repressed memory, but some
perverseness keeps me going back to name
those sadnesses as if my tongue
could cure by catalogue, as if a song
were all that was needed against the pain
of having been so lost—the redwing's gone—

*

taking his song along. Now all that's left
is that awful silence, which as a girl
I was taught to fill up with pretty talk
so as to make everyone comfortable;
the kind of talk that is equivalent
to vacuum cleaner noise, sucks everything
interesting out of talk and isn't meant
to ease a three o'clock in the morning
terror, say. Against such talk I write—
or try to anyway—that other kind
of talk that is as awful as silence
if it hits the mark, when just the right
string of words will make your life fall in line
and shine with an eloquent radiance.

*

Just the other night at a reception
I was politely working my way out
after fulfilling the obligation
that had brought me there. Oh dreary night!
I was ready for stars, a heady rain
or cool breeze tangling my skirt in my legs—
when a Fred or a Tom, a nametag name,
came up to me. I'm not sure what he said
but with a few questions he'd taken us
deep into the spell of the night going on
outside those closed windows. I could have wept
for finding at long last this oasis
of real talk. The breeze blew in. The stars came on
inside that room. I thanked him when I left.

*

I was driving somewhere far with a friend,
some talk was going on: she said, I said—
the kind of conversation rightly penned
dialogue in the handbooks. Then instead
of her next cue, she asked me what I thought
of her, *really* thought. Oh Jesus, I thought,
we still have a long ways to go and what
do I know what she means to do with what
I tell her. Use it so sue me?! Call it
a risk I took or say that small Tercel
drove me to higher ground. I told the truth
mostly, as Huck says, then asked what she thought
of me. I could've stopped the car right there
as this was where we'd wanted to get to.

*

I brought a record of common birdsongs
so as to learn to tell the birds apart,
but I gave up trying to follow along.
I'd have one bird down, say, a meadowlark,
chee-up-trill. But right on its tailfeathers
came the peewee with its *pee-ah-wee*,
exactly like the *zee-zee* of the warbler
or the *drink your tea* (so it sounded to me)
of the towhee. Finally, to top it all,
the mockingbird mimicking everyone.
It was bird-Babel worse than biblical
to human ears, which should humble us some
to think our poems no more than mating trills
for the birds: *whan-that-aprill, whan-that-aprill.*

*

I had this friend—we were always talking.
She'd come over or I'd go to her place
and as she let me in we'd start talking
up the stairs to her flat. I was amazed
we ever got sat down with coffee cups
in our hands or ever stopped our talking
long enough to drink what was in those cups.
We'd take a walk and suddenly look up
lost, but finish our points before trying
to discuss our way back. Were we crazy
binge-talkers or sensing the imminence
of what became our lives' parting, maybe
we were preparing then for this silence?

*

I've heard said that among the eskimos
there are over a hundred words for snow:
the soft kind, the hard-driving kind, the roll
a snowball kind: snow being such a force
in their lives, it needs a blizzard of words.
In my own D.R. we have many rains:
the sprinkle, the shower, the hurricane,
the tears, the many tears for our many dead.
I've asked around and find that in all tongues
there are at least a dozen words for talk:
the heart-to-heart, the chat, the confession,
the juicy gossip, the quip, the harangue—
no matter where we're from we need to talk
about snow, rain, about being human.

*

Only a few times has talk failed me,
times when I realized nothing that I said
or heard would help, when I felt I could be
talking outside my species, times the dead
would have made more involved listeners, times
I could tell by the narrowed eyes, cocked head
that all I said was being ground down fine,
then mixed with shards of mistrust to be fed
right back to me, while the same marinade
was stewing inside me. I don't know how
to turn a talk around once it goes bad.
Sometimes I think of writing as a way
of going back to those failures and somehow
saying exactly what I wish I'd said.

*

He's back—perched on the line—not just a song
from some distracting whatchamacallit,
but obvious in his glossy uniform—
which might explain why he's my favorite,
recalling with his gorgeous epaulettes
my childhood in a dictatorship
when real talk was punishable by death,
though some—like him—refused such censorship.
As now he belts his song, breaking the hold
of that past as his *compañeros* come,
a regiment on the line, all going strong,
affirming that the saying of the world
is what we're meant to do with chirps or words.
So you take it from here, redwing blackbirds!

*

LAST NIGHT
AT TÍA'S

Last Night at Tía's

The night before I left the capital
to go back to my husband in Vermont,
the cousins gathered at Tía Rosa's house
to say goodbye—the whole blood entourage
of grown and glamorous Dominicans
with children whose fresh faces echoed theirs
as I remembered them from childhood.
Remember ... remember was now the theme
of all our conversations, the thread holding
together what was left of our connection.

The jasmine blossoms spilled their strong perfume
in the garden whose deepening shadows
we watched surround us on the patio.
A cousin pointed out the flamboyant
I could barely make out, remembering
how we'd climb up to the highest branches
gathering the long black pods before they dropped
for points in a game I had forgotten.
Who was the best behaved? Who was naughty?
(Why did I feel the urge to call out, Me?)

In the distance Columbus's lighthouse
began flashing its costly cross of light
into the sky. Someone pointed it out
as proud proof of our Spanish ancestry.
I kept quiet knowing our differences
in point of view could snap the fragile thread
that held us there and sour the evening
I needed to take back with me. A word
could snuff the stars that seemed more luminous
in skies left over from my childhood.

The children ran shrieking in the garden,
followed by tired maids who cautioned them
against hurting themselves, scolds seconded
without much conviction by their mothers,
who feelingly kissed away new scratches,
scolding the maids for lack of watchfulness.
The male cousins bragged about their sons—
accomplishments that far outdistanced ours
at that same age. Who was there to correct
the exaggerations of memory?

Or who would want to at this late hour
among the orchids basking in moonlight
in baskets Tía's daughters buy for her
on Tío's birthday each year since his death.
(Who would have thought Tío would go so young?)
But it was other deaths besides the dead
we mourned: a grand old family far-flung—
Papito's mind gone, Tití in New York;
we lost-sheep sisters married and divorced
so frequently the family tree has been

cluttered with spouses instead of children;
our nanny's grandkids now *minorities*
in the U.S. with first-rate scholarships
to the best colleges—a pregnant sigh—
I did not labor into confession
since I could sense the losses that we mourned
were different but proceeded from one cause:
the past was over—the old ones were gone—
and Columbus's lighted cross beckoned
like the first star in a childhood sky,

the one we used to wish by for a future
not unlike this one, give or take a few
sadnesses and ex-husbands, give or take
mistakes from the expected (naughty) ones
everyone was kind enough not to mention.
We had become *the grown-ups* to our young,
readying ourselves for the big deaths: our own,
with the future shrieking in the garden,
and the lighthouse beaming its useless light
above the dark we had to navigate

down the garden path to the swimming pool
where the nightblooming cereus were opening
their flowers in slow motion to the moon,
dozens of them Tía snapped from their stalks
and set afloat like fragrant caravels
on their brief journeys. It seemed each of us
was one of those frail boats the children tried
to steer with splashes—but it was too late.
We had already strayed from that old world
of the past we had shared with each other.

AFTERWORD

Coming Home to *Homecoming*

I remember the night I got my box of twenty-five copies of *Homecoming*. My first book! I had just come home from teaching a late workshop. It was almost midnight, that witching time for ambitious girls with plans. And there it was by my door, a box from Grove publishers. I pushed it indoors, opened it, sat down on it, and read. What had I done? I had gone public with a voice! I was excited, I was scared, I wasn't sure I shouldn't hide my face until all the books out there were sold and forgotten.

Now twelve years later, rereading *Homecoming*, I wonder what all that fuss was about. The confessions of my young woman's voice seem so fresh and tentative—who would they have offended? It pains me, too, that I had no sooner achieved a voice but I wanted to silence her. Even now, three books braver, I think of that young woman so often when I write. I am still she, heart pounding in my chest, wondering, Do I dare?

Where did that young woman's fears come from? Nothing in my Dominican background had prepared me for what I was doing—having a voice, and in English, no less! The only models I had been given by my mother and aunts and the heroines of novels were the homemaking model and the romantic model, both of which I had miserably failed at by age thirty-four.

So you see, what shocked me that midnight was that I heard my own voice loud and clear. And it spooked me. Once I said a little, I could say so much. So I sat on that box, as if to keep the lid on that voice.

But it was too late. I had already set her loose. She had a life of her own, she grew, she gained ground. She went into fiction. And in returning to this book, she had new things to say and little revisions to make.

For instance. In writing *Homecoming*, I can see now how fiercely I was claiming my woman's voice. As I followed my mother cleaning house, washing and ironing clothes, rolling dough, I was using the material of my housebound girl life to claim my woman's legacy. Still, it amazes me how little I dared speak of some of the confusions and complications of that legacy. And so, in some of the new poems in this section—"Charges," "Folding My Clothes," and "Mother Love" especially—I address aspects of being my mother's daughter that my young woman's voice could not speak.

Something else. In trying to find the voice that the speaker of "33" so anxiously searches for, I could not admit the further confusions of my bilingual, bicultural self. Except for "Homecoming," the poem that opened the original book, I did not address my experience as a Dominican-American woman. Indeed, that earlier voice did not even feel permission to do so, as if to call attention to my foreignness would make my readers question my right to write in English.

In tinkering with *Homecoming* for this new edition, I decided to respect for the most part the locutions and circumlocutions of that young woman's voice. Only in a few instances, I couldn't help myself. I allowed that young Latina her little bits of Spanish, a *tía* here, a *Mami* there. And to the birthday poem, "33," written during my thirty-third year, I added new sonnets to add up to my age this year of publication, forty-six. These additions reflect a political awareness absent, for the most part, in the young woman of thirty-three.

But why come back to these old poems at all? This book is where I started: in these poems that claimed my woman's legacy and my vocation as a writer. It heartens me that twelve years later coming home to *Homecoming*, I feel so at home with the young woman's voice of these poems. I am glad she spoke up. In part, it is she I am celebrating in the new sonnet sequence, "Redwing Sonnets." These ten poems speak of the healing art of talking, of the power of the word that can topple dictatorships or name the world. And, finally, I take her "home" again to the island in "Last Night at Tía's," though by now she surely knows where her roots really are—deep in the terra firma of the language.